SAMUEL BARBER
Hermit Songs, Op. 29

Edited by Richard Walters

ED 2177

ISBN 978-0-4803-9516-9

G. SCHIRMER, Inc.

DISTRIBUTED BY

HAL•LEONARD®
CORPORATION
7777 W. BLUEMOUND RD. P.O. BOX 13819 MILWAUKEE, WI 53213

www.musicsalesclassical.com
www.halleonard.com

CONTENTS

HERMIT SONGS, Op. 29

Published by G. Schirmer, 1954. Composed November 1952 to February 1953. The cycle was commissioned by the Elizabeth Sprague Coolidge Foundation, to be performed on the occasion of the Annual Founder's Day Concert. Elizabeth Sprague Coolidge (1864-1953) was an heiress and music lover whose foundation was, in part, devoted to the encouragement of chamber music, especially championing contemporary composers. The illustrious list of composers who benefitted from the Coolidge Foundation included Bartók, Bloch, Britten, Copland, Hindemith, Martinů, Milhaud, Poulenc, Prokofiev, Respighi, Ravel, Schoenberg and Stravinsky. She donated funds to the Library of Congress for its Coolidge Auditorium. *Hermit Songs* was premiered there by soprano Leontyne Price and Barber on October 30, 1953, just five days before Elizabeth Coolidge's death.

As composition began in November 1952, Barber wrote to his composer uncle, Sidney Homer:

> I have come across some poems of the 10th century, translated into modern English by various people, and am making a song cycle of them, to be called, perhaps "Hermit Songs." These were extraordinary men, monks or hermits or what not, and they wrote these little poems on the corners of MSS they were illuminating or just copying. I find them very direct, unspoiled and often curiously contemporaneous in feeling.

In the same letter Barber wrote out the texts of the songs. After the last (the song which was later titled "The Desire for Hermitage"), Barber wrote:

> Dear Uncle, do not take the last one literally; I am not that much of a Hermit, for I have just rented a little apartment in New York, having decided that there is some life in the old dog yet.

The original G. Schirmer edition of *Hermit Songs* included the following introduction, written by Barber:

> The *Hermit Songs*, commissioned by the Elizabeth Sprague Coolidge Foundation, were first performed by Leontyne Price, soprano, with the composer at the piano, at the Library of Congress, Washington, D.C., on October 30, 1953. They are settings of anonymous Irish texts of the eighth to thirteenth centuries written by monks and scholars, often on the margins of the manuscripts they were copying or illuminating — perhaps not always meant to be seen by their Father Superiors. They are small poems, thoughts or observations, some very short, and speak in straightforward, droll, and often surprisingly modern terms of the simple life these men led, close to nature, to animals and to God. Some are literal translations and others, where existing translations seemed inadequate, were especially made by W.H. Auden and Chester Kallman. Robin Flower in *The Irish Tradition* has written as follows: "It was not only that these scribes and anchorites lived by the destiny of their dedication in an environment of wood and sea; it was because they brought into that environment an eye washed miraculously clear by a continual spiritual exercise that they, first in Europe, had that strange vision of natural things in an almost unnatural purity."

The published introduction to the original edition continues with a quotation from *Stories from Keating's History of Ireland*, edited by Osborn Bergin, a passage chosen by Barber:

> Mochua and Columcille lived at the same time and Mochua, being a hermit in the waste, had no worldly goods but only a cock, a mouse and a fly. And the office of the cock was to keep the hour of matins for him. As for the mouse it would never suffer him to sleep but five hours, day and night, and if he was like to sleep longer, being weary with vigils and prostrations, the mouse would fall to licking his ear till it woke him. And the fly's office was to be walking along each line of his psalter as he read it, and when he was weary with singing his psalms, the fly would abide upon the line where he left off until he could return again to the saying of the psalms. Now it came to pass that these three precious ones died soon. And upon that Mochua wrote a letter to Columcille in Alba, sorrowing for the death of his flock. Columcille replied to him and this is what he said: "My brother," he said, "marvel not that thy flock should have died, for misfortune ever waits upon wealth."

Solitude and aloneness were a theme of Barber's life and work. He craved silence and solitude for composition, and preferred the country to the city. The separated individual appears in various meaning and contexts in other Barber works beyond *Hermit Songs*: "With rue my heart is laden," "Bessie Bobtail," "A Nun Takes the Veil," "Sure on this shining night," "Despite and Still" and "Solitary Hotel." James Agee's text for *Knoxville: Summer of 1915* is certainly about an individual's inevitable aloneness, though not in actual solitude. And in the opera *Vanessa*, the title character's seclusion is related to the same theme.

Barber's Irish heritage steered him to Irish poetry as early as the 1920s, and Irish literature remained an interest, though he had not traveled to Ireland. In the summer of 1952 Barber made a trip to Donegal, where he delighted in reading Yeats. The composer discovered that Yeats' grave was surrounded by tombstones of Barbers, possibly his unknown distant relatives. The choice of medieval Irish texts for *Hermit Songs* certainly seems related to the Irish trip a few months before composition.

The songs were not actually composed for Leontyne Price. In a letter of May, 1953 he describes the completed songs and adds, "but haven't found the ideal singer yet." Price was a student of Florence Page Kimball, a friend of Barber's. Barber and Menotti heard Price in Kimball's studio in May or June of 1953 in an informal recital of her students. Price's rise to fame was still ahead of her, and she had never sung a professional recital. Barber gave Price the cycle to learn, but still floundered about the choice of singer. In a letter of July 24, 1953 to William Strickland Barber writes:

> Do you know the soprano [Irmgard] Seefried? I have sent her my Hermit Songs to look over; they are to be sung by someone in October at the Library of Congress. I do not know whether Seefried is the right one or not, I love her singing but have never met her and do not know how good her English is. She is supposed to be a delightful person. Maybe you would meet her and play them with her, although I am sure she is very busy with the Salzburg season. The negro soprano, Leontyne Price—very talented—is learning them here and I shall hear them next week. Do you know the baritone Fischer-Dieskau?

It is interesting to note that Barber's concept for the premiere of *Hermit Songs* was not necessarily for soprano, indicated by his interest in Dietrich Fischer-Dieskau (for whom he would later write a set of songs). Barber was not opposed to transpositions of his songs, even for first performances. Eleanor Steber was apparently considered briefly for *Hermit Songs*, but Price obviously impressed Barber. She must have sung the cycle that August in her teacher's studio for him. The composer William Schuman, Barber's exact contemporary and then the president of the Juilliard School, recalled in a 1981 interview:

> I was at the first performance of the *Hermit Songs* given by Leontyne Price at the home of her teacher Florence Page Kimball with Barber at the piano. That was one of the great experiences I recall of hearing new music.

By the end of the summer Barber had written of Price, "she does them beautifully; it is a beautiful voice." Price and Barber collaborated closely after *Hermit Songs*, and remained friends until his death. He composed the opera *Antony and Cleopatra* for her, and the cycle *Despite and Still*. Price very frequently performed Barber songs on her many recitals. Other Barber songs were performed by Price and Barber at the Library of Congress premiere of *Hermit Songs*, including "The Daisies," "Nocturne," "Sleep Now" and "Nuvoletta."

Price and Barber were invited to perform *Hermit Songs* at the Twentieth-Century Music Conference in Rome in April, 1954. In liner notes to the compilation recording "Modern American Vocal Works," which includes *Hermit Songs*, Ned Rorem wrote of his personal memories of the performance:

> In the Roman spring of 1954, for a fortnight we attended concert after charmless concert of the dead-serious and absurdly complex efforts of Boulez's acolytes. How Samuel Barber came to be invited is anyone's guess. Yet suddenly one Tuesday, when we had grown bug-eyed at the gravity of it all, onto the stage came Sam to accompany the unknown Leontyne Price, every inch a diva with her azure sequins, in Hermit Songs. From the first bars of "At Saint Patrick's Purgatory" the all-knowing audience exchanged glances: you don't compose trash like this anymore. Still, the glamorous dynamism of Leontyne was hard to scorn — nothing like it had ever been experienced on land or sea. But when the hit song "The Monk and His Cat" came round there were audible hisses, and the close of the cycle brought loud boos mixed with furtive cheers. Yet who today recalls the other programs? While the Hermit Songs prevail. Separately and as a group they are perfection, being technically what singers like to wrap their tongues around, and emotionally both broad and precise.

Price made her New York recital debut in November, 1954, again singing *Hermit Songs*, with Barber at the piano. Alvin Ailey choreographed a 1961 solo ballet to the cycle, which he danced himself.

At Saint Patrick's Purgatory
words 13th century Gaelic, anonymous, translated by Sean O'Faolain

Composed on November 17, 1952.

Church Bell at Night
words 12th century Gaelic, anonymous, translated by Howard Mumford Jones

Composed on November 3, 1952.

St. Ita's Vision
words attributed to Saint Ita, 8th century Gaelic, translated by Chester Kallman

Composed on January 9, 1953.

The Heavenly Banquet

words attributed to St. Brigid, 10th century Gaelic, translated by Sean O'Faolain

Composed on November 13, 1952.

The Crucifixion

words 12th century anonymous Gaelic from *The Speckled Book*, translated by Howard Mumford Jones

Composed on October 26, 1952.

Sea-Snatch

words 8th or 9th century Gaelic, anonymous, translated by Kenneth Jackson

Composed on January 6, 1953.

Promiscuity

words 9th century Gaelic, anonymous, translated by Kenneth Jackson

Composed on January 15, 1953.

The Monk and His Cat

words 8th or 9th century Gaelic, anonymous, translated by W.H. Auden

Composed on February 16, 1953. Dedicated to Isabelle Vengerova, a gift for her seventy-sixth birthday. Vengerova was Barber's piano teacher at Curtis. A legendary presence there, her students included Leonard Bernstein, Lukas Foss, Leonard Pennario, Gary Graffman and Abbey Simon. Barber adapted the song for SATB chorus and piano.

The Praises of God

words 11th century Gaelic, anonymous, translated by W.H. Auden

Composed on January 27, 1953. Dedicated to the memory of Mary Evans Scott.

The Desire for Hermitage

words 8th or 9th century Gaelic, anonymous, translated by Sean O'Faolain, altered by S.B.

Composed on January 15, 1953.

— Richard Walters

The sources for all quotations from Samuel Barber's diary and letters are two books by Barbara Heyman, *Samuel Barber: The Composer and His Music* (Oxford University Press, 1992), and *Samuel Barber: A Thematic Catalogue of the Complete Works* (Oxford University Press, 2012).

VOCAL TEXTS

I. At Saint Patrick's Purgatory
13th century
Translated by Sean O'Faolain

Pity me on my pilgrimage to Loch Derg!*
O King of the churches and the bells
bewailing your sores and your wounds,
But not a tear can I squeeze from my eyes!
Not moisten an eye after so much sin!
Pity me, O King!
What shall I do with a heart that seeks only its own ease?
O only begotten Son by whom all men were made,
who shunned not the death by three wounds,
pity me on my pilgrimage to Loch Derg
and I with a heart not softer than a stone!

II. Church Bell at Night
12th century
Translated by Howard Mumford Jones

Sweet little bell, struck on a windy night,
I would liefer keep tryst with thee
Than be
With a light and foolish woman.

III. St. Ita's Vision
Attributed to Saint Ita, 8th century
Translated by Chester Kallman

"I will take nothing from my Lord," said she,
"unless He gives me His Son from Heaven
In the form of a Baby that I may nurse Him."
So that Christ came down to her
in the form of a Baby and then she said:
"Infant Jesus, at my breast,
Nothing in this world is true
Save, O tiny nursling, You.
Infant Jesus, at my breast,
By my heart every night,
You I nurse are not
A churl but were begot
On Mary the Jewess by Heaven's Light.
Infant Jesus, at my breast,
what King is there but You who could
Give everlasting Good?
wherefor I give my food.
Sing to Him, maidens, sing your best!
There is none that has such right
To your song as Heaven's King
Who every night
Is Infant Jesus at my breast."

IV. The Heavenly Banquet
Attributed to St. Brigid, 10th century
Translated by Sean O'Faolain

I would like to have the men of Heaven in my own house;
with vats of good cheer laid out for them.
I would like to have the three Marys, their fame is so great.
I would like people from every corner of Heaven.
I would like them to be cheerful in their drinking.
I would like to have Jesus sitting here among them.
I would like a great lake of beer for the King of Kings.
I would like to be watching Heaven's family
Drinking it through all eternity.

V. The Crucifixion
From The Speckled Book, 12th century
Translated by Howard Mumford Jones

At the cry of the first bird
They began to crucify Thee, O Swan!
Never shall lament cease because of that.
It was like the parting of day from night.
Ah, sore was the suffering borne
By the body of Mary's Son,
But sorer still to Him was the grief
Which for His sake
Came upon His Mother.

VI. Sea-Snatch
8th-9th century

It has broken us, it has crushed us, it has drowned us,
O King of the starbright Kingdom of Heaven;
the wind has consumed us, swallowed us,
as timber is devoured by crimson fire from Heaven.
It has broken us, it has crushed us, it has drowned us,
O King of the starbright Kingdom of Heaven!

VII. Promiscuity
9th century

I do not know with whom Edan will sleep,
but I do know that fair Edan will not sleep alone.

---

* Loch Derg (Red Lake) in County Donegal has been a place of
pilgrimage form very early times.

VIII. The Monk and His Cat

8th or 9th century
Translated by W.H. Auden

Pangur, white Pangur,
How happy we are
Alone together,
Scholar and cat.
Each has his own work to do daily;
For you it is hunting, for me study.
Your shining eye watches the wall;
my feeble eye is fixed on a book.
You rejoice when your claws
Entrap a mouse;
I rejoice when my mind
Fathoms a problem.
Pleased with his own art,
Neither hinders the other;
Thus we live ever
Without tedium and envy.
Pangur, white Pangur,
How happy we are
Alone together,
Scholar and cat.

IX. The Praises of God

11th century
Translated by W.H. Auden

How foolish the man
Who does not raise
His voice and praise
With joyful words,
As he alone can,
Heaven's High King.
To Whom the light birds
With no soul but air,
All day, everywhere
Laudation sing.

X. The Desire for Hermitage

8th-9th century
Based on a translation by Sean O'Faolain

Ah! to be all alone in a little cell with nobody near me;
beloved that pilgrimage before the last pilgrimage to Death.
Singing the passing hours to cloudy Heaven;
feeding upon dry bread and water from the cold spring.
That will be an end to evil when I am alone
in a lovely little corner among tombs
far from the houses of the great.
Ah! to be all alone in a little cell,
to be alone, all alone:
Alone I came into the world,
alone I shall go from it.

Hermit Songs

To Elizabeth Sprague Coolidge

I. At Saint Patrick's Purgatory

original key: G-sharp minor

13th century
Translated by Sean O'Faolain

Samuel Barber
Op. 29, No. 1
1952

*Loch Derg (Red Lake) in County Donegal has been a place of pilgrimage from very early times.

But not _ a tear _____ can I squeeze from my eyes! _____

Not mois - ten an eye _____ af -ter so ____ much sin! Pi -ty me, _ O

King! _____ What shall I do with a heart that seeks _ on-ly its

own ease? _____ O _____ on -ly be-got-ten Son

Nov. 17, 1952

II. Church Bell at Night
original key

12th century
Translated by Howard Mumford Jones

Samuel Barber
Op. 29, No. 2
1952

Molto adagio ♩ = 46

Sweet lit - tle bell, struck on a wind - y night,

I would lie - fer keep tryst with thee Than be

With a light and fool - ish wo - man.

Text from *Romanesque Lyric,* by permission of the University of North Carolina Press.

Nov. 3, 1952

III. St. Ita's* Vision

original key: a major second higher

Attributed to Saint Ita, 8th century
Translated by Chester Kallman

Samuel Barber
Op. 29, No. 3
1953

*Ita – pronounce Eeta
**Printed as a C-natural in the first edition.
Words used by special permission.

Andante con moto ♩. = 46

"In - fant Je - sus, at my — breast, Noth-ing in this world is true

Save, O ti - ny nurs - ling, You. In - fant Je - sus, at my — breast,

By my heart ev - 'ry night, You I nurse are not A churl but were be-got On

Ma - ry the Jew-ess by Heav - en's Light. In - fant Je - sus,

at my ___ breast, what King is there but You who could

Give ev - er-last - ing Good? where - for ___ I ___ give my ___ food. ___

Sing to Him, maid - ens, sing your __ best! There is none that has such right __ To your song as Heav - en's King Who ev - 'ry night __ Is In - fant Je - sus at my __ breast, at my __ breast."

cresc. molto

f

f *molto sonoro*

r.h. *l.h.*

non arpeg.

sim.

p *rall.* *p* *a tempo, senza rall.*

p *rall.* *p* *a tempo, senza rall.*

8ba

pp *Ped.*

pp

l.h.

Jan. 9, 1953

IV. The Heavenly Banquet

original key: a major second higher

Attributed to Saint Brigid, 10th century
Translated by Sean O'Faolain

Samuel Barber
Op. 29, No. 4
1952

Lively, with good humor ♩ = 108

I would like to have the men of Heav - en in my own

house; with vats of good cheer laid out for them. I would like to have the three

Mar - ys, their fame is so great. I would like peo - ple from ev - 'ry

Text from *The Silver Branch* by Sean O'Faolain, copyright 1938, by the Viking Press, Inc., by permission of The Viking Press, Inc., New York, and Jonathan Cape Limited, London.

In the first edition several L.H. chords were altered by Barber to avoid awkward fingering in this transposition. We have reprinted the alterations. Affected measures: 2, 4, 6, 8, 9, 11, 13, 14, 24, 25, 30, 32.

I would like to be watch-ing Heav - en's

fam - i - ly   Drink-ing it through all e - ter - ni - ty.

Nov. 13, 1952

V. The Crucifixion

original key: a major second higher

From The Speckled Book, 12th Century
Translated by Howard Mumford Jones

Samuel Barber
Op. 29, No. 5
1952

At the cry of the first bird They be-gan to cru-ci-fy Thee, O Swan! Nev-er shall la-ment cease be-cause of that. It was like the part-ing of day from night.

sost. ped.

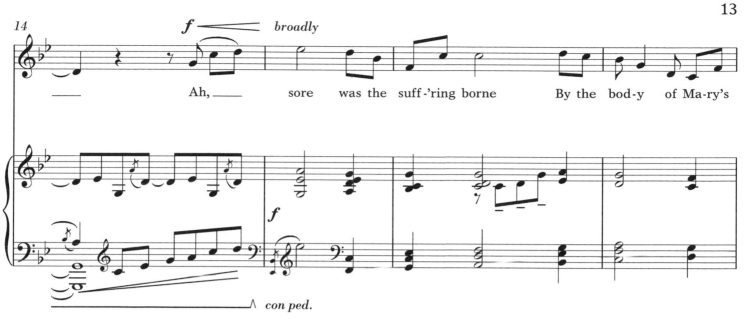

Ah, _____ sore was the suff-'ring borne By the bod-y of Ma-ry's

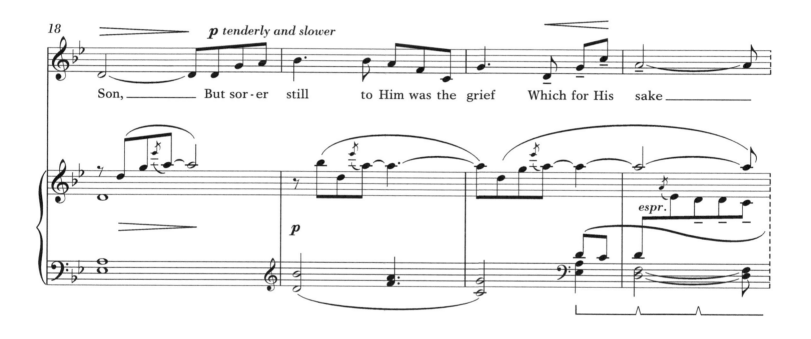

Son, _____ But sor - er still to Him was the grief Which for His sake _____

Tempo I

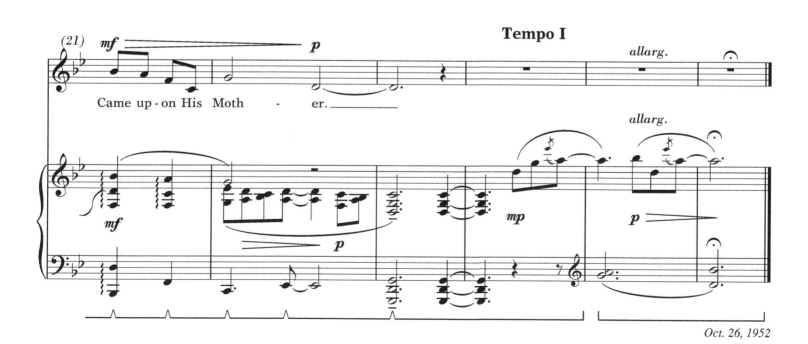

Came up - on His Moth - er. _____

Oct. 26, 1952

VI. Sea-Snatch
original key: C minor

8th–9th century
Translated by Kenneth Jackson

Samuel Barber
Op. 29, No. 6
1953

Text from Kenneth Jackson's *A Celtic Miscellany,* by permission of Routledge and Kegan Paul, Ltd., London, and Harvard University Press, Cambridge, Mass.

*Barber altered the grace note in the transposed lower key.

**Barber altered the final two chords in the transposed lower key because of the range of the piano.

Jan. 6, 1953

VII. Promiscuity
original key

9th century
Translated by Kenneth Jackson

Samuel Barber
Op. 29, No. 7
1953

Jan. 15, 1953

Text from Kenneth Jackson's *A Celtic Miscellany,* by permission of Routledge and Kegan Paul, Ltd., London, and Harvard University Press, Cambridge, Mass.

*Edan: pronounce Ay-den.

To Isabelle Vengerova

VIII. The Monk and His Cat
original key

8th or 9th century
Translated by W.H. Auden

Samuel Barber
Op. 29, No. 8
1953

Words used by special permission.

*Notes marked (−) in these two measures should be slightly longer, pochissimo rubato; also on the fourth page. [Barber's footnote]

I re-joice when my mind Fath-oms a prob-lem.

Pleased with his own art, _____ Neith-er hin - ders the oth - er; _

_____ Thus we live e - ver _____ With-out te - dium and en - vy. _____

Pan-gur, white Pan - gur, _

Feb. 16, 1953

To the memory of Mary Evans Scott

IX. The Praises of God

original key: a major second higher

11th century
Translated by W.H. Auden

Samuel Barber
Op. 29, No. 9
1953

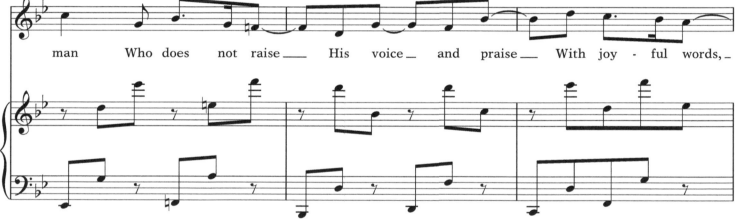

Words used by special permission.

22

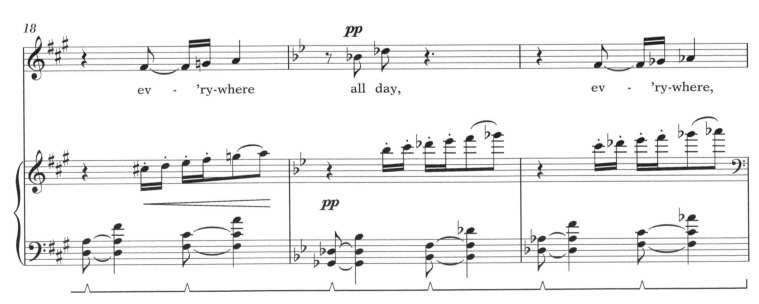

*Pedal markings in measures 17–20 are for the sostenuto pedal.

Jan. 27, 1953

X. The Desire for Hermitage

original key: a major second higher

8th–9th century
Based on a translation by Sean O'Faolain

Samuel Barber
Op. 29, No. 10
1953

Text from *The Silver Branch* by Sean O'Faolain, copyright 1938 by The Viking Press, Inc., by permission of The Viking Press, Inc., New York, and Jonathan Cape Limited, London.
*All grace-notes somewhat longer, rubato. [Barber's footnote]

Jan. 15, 1953